Original title:
The Cherries of Change

Copyright © 2025 Creative Arts Management OÜ
All rights reserved.

Author: Gideon Shaw
ISBN HARDBACK: 978-1-80586-283-3
ISBN PAPERBACK: 978-1-80586-755-5

Petal by Petal

Dropping petals like confetti,
Sprung from branches, oh so yeti.
Sipping nectar, feeling bright,
Bumblebees buzzing, what a sight!

Dance around with ants in tow,
Tickled toes on grass below.
Petals party, what a thrill,
Nature's laughter is the real deal!

Fruits of the Moment

Bananas slip in tiny shoes,
Laughing loudly, sharing news.
Apples toss their seeds in jest,
While grapes play hide and seek, oh yes!

Fruits are mocking, ripe with glee,
Jokes unravel from every tree.
Each bite's a giggle, juicy cheer,
As nature's whimsy draws us near!

Nature's Palette

Colors clash in leafy glee,
Crayons spill from every tree.
Flowers giggle in the sun,
Each bloom bursting, oh what fun!

Green and gold, a vibrant mess,
Nature's brush, no need to stress.
Painted skies and playful breeze,
Artisans of joy, if you please!

A Harvest of New Ideas

Harvest moon, a playful sight,
Cabbages wearing hats so tight.
Carrots chat with dainty peas,
Sharing secrets with the breeze.

Onions giggle, crying tears,
Lettuce laughing through the years.
Ideas sprout like beans in row,
In this patch, creativity flows!

Beneath the Blossoms of Transformation

Beneath the trees in a wild dance,
A squirrel laughs at its own prance.
Pink petals flutter, oh what a sight,
They tickle the clouds, feeling just right.

Each blossom a matter of whimsy and cheer,
As birds chirp nonsense, loud and clear.
A breeze carries giggles through the green maze,
Nature's comedy unfolds in delightful ways.

Red Fruit Beneath Shifting Skies

Beneath a sky that's looking quite mad,
The fruit are blushing, all feeling glad.
Bouncing about on branches so spry,
Laughing at raindrops that fall from the sky.

They trade jokes with bees who buzz in delight,
While ants march in lines, all ready to bite.
The reds and the greens in a jovial race,
Nature's capers with a funny face.

Sweetness in Seasons of Shift

When springtime giggles march into view,
Swapping their coats for a bright shade of blue.
Laughter erupts with a twist and a turn,
As each little fruit takes a turn to discern.

Through tangles of leaves, the whispers arise,
Chasing each other with curious eyes.
In this carnival of bud and bloom,
Every silly joke chases away the gloom.

A Harvest of New Beginnings

In gardens where laughter sprouts like weeds,
A parade of new fruits fulfilling our needs.
With every pluck, a giggle and cheer,
As creatures in frocks all join in the sphere.

The harvest is merry, the baskets are bright,
Fruit juggling contests last day and night.
With games and tomfoolery filling the air,
In this orchard of joy, there's always a flair.

Lessons Growing on the Vine

In a garden, wisdom blooms,
Picking laughs from leafy rooms.
Every fruit a lesson learned,
With each bite, a joy returned.

Swinging high on branches wide,
Learning how to take the ride.
Buds of laughter in the air,
Life's a joke if you don't care.

Seeds of Revolution in the Orchard

Apples plotting on the ground,
Grapes are giggling all around.
A pear in riot, who would guess?
Fruitful chaos, what a mess!

Berries masked in shades of green,
Planning pranks, a fruity scene.
Rebellion rooted oh so deep,
In this orchard, secrets creep.

The Flavor of Tomorrow's Dreams

Taste the wild, a future bright,
Ripe with laughter, pure delight.
Sour notes turn sweet, you see,
All it takes is some esprit.

Whiff of dreams on petals light,
Fruits of hope in morning's sight.
Bite the zest, you'll feel the wave,
Life's a feast, be bold and brave.

Turn of the Seasons, Turn of the Heart

When winter ends, springs frolic cheer,
A cabbage joins, it's rather weird.
Every frost a chuckle mild,
Nature's giggles, sweet and wild.

Leaves like confetti swirl and twirl,
In a dance, watch nature whirl.
Hearts in bloom, feel the delight,
Seasons shift with a playful bite.

Joys of Emergence

In springtime's light, the buds explode,
A squirrel slips by with a funny load.
Giggling leaves dance in the breeze,
While bees throw parties atop the trees.

With laughter sprouting from blooms so bright,
A garden of chuckles, what a sight!
Worms wearing hats wiggle with pride,
As laughter erupts from the garden side.

A Symphony of Seasons

Winter whispers, 'I need a break,'
While the snowman jokes, 'I'm made of flake!'
Spring tunes up with a floral band,
Making rhymes with a cheeky hand.

As summer slides in, it hiccups a bit,
Sunshine and ice cream, a perfect fit.
Autumn rolls by with a bellyache,
From all the pies it couldn't forsake.

The Scent of Progress

Fresh grass smells like a comic strip,
While daisies giggle in a joyful quip.
Pollen's a prankster, flying about,
Allergies laughing with a big shout.

In gardens where giggles sprout and thrive,
A ladybug wears shades, feeling alive.
Each seed in soil tells a joke anew,
As nature grows wild, in shades of hue.

Nature's Rebirth

From dirt comes laughter, a sprout so bold,
Petals unfolding like stories told.
The sun pops in with a wink and a grin,
As life sneaks out with a dance and spin.

Critters caper, in their playful way,
Chasing the shadows of yesterday.
With every bloom, a giggle and tease,
Nature's a jester, with joy to please.

Pathways of Ripening

In a garden, red fruits gleam,
With whispers of a silly dream.
They bounce around with glee and cheer,
Each one thinking it's a seer.

A wobbly tree with branches wide,
Where giggles mix with juicy pride.
The squirrels dance, the rabbits sing,
Oh, what joy the harvest can bring!

Interludes of Evolution

A plump one pats its buddy, 'Look!'
'This old vine gives a funny nook!'
They scheme to roll and frolic far,
While dreaming of their own sweet jar.

A bird's-eye view of ripening fun,
As laughter bursts beneath the sun.
They blush and giggle, what a scene,
As petals dance in joyful sheen!

Branches of Journey

Off they sway, the fruits in glee,
With stories brewed from the old tree.
A beetle struts with shiny pride,
Saying, 'I'm more than just a ride!'

Each branch a tale, each leaf a joke,
As nature ebbs with playful poke.
They roll and bounce, they leap so high,
As cloud-sheep float in the blue sky!

Radiance in Transition

As colors blend in summer's light,
The fruits giggle, feeling just right.
They bump and jostle, 'Let it rain!'
In nature's dance, they feel no pain.

The sunbeams play, the shadows tease,
With bursts of laughter on the breeze.
In every ripening, a cheeky grin,
For all know change is where it begins!

Seeds of Alteration

In gardens wild, we toss our seeds,
Hoping for growth—oh, what wild leads!
A carrot here, a turnip there,
Who knew potatoes could dance in the air?

We plant our dreams with silly glee,
A llama jumps—'What's wrong with me?'
With every sprout, we laugh and vie,
For vegetables that pretend to fly.

The Dance of Renewal

The sun spills laughter on the ground,
As veggies waltz, round and round!
Cabbages twirl in a jolly spree,
While radishes shimmy like they're on spree.

The spinach sings a high-pitched tune,
Bouncing around like a loony balloon!
As peas do pirouettes, oh what a sight,
Every sprout jives, till it's well past night.

Spontaneous Blooming

From cracks in the pavement, blooms burst forth,
A dandelion's disco, proving its worth!
With petals like confetti, oh what a bash,
As bees join the fray with a buzzing splash.

Funny little daisies wear tops like a crown,
Chasing the winds, spinning round and down!
In this quirk of nature, we all share a grin,
As flowers gather for a wild pollen spin.

Fading Shadows

As daylight wanes, shadows creep,
Those cheeky plants in corners peep!
"Hide, here comes the pruner!" they squeak,
As leaves hold meetings, gossiping sneak.

The raspberries shiver; they're quite the fright,
"Don't clip my buds; I'm not ready for night!"
Yet every shadow holds a truth so bright,
In fading laughter lies the best insight.

Brightening Light

When morning giggles chase away the night,
Tiny buds awaken, filled with delight.
Their colors burst forth like laughter's refrain,
Tickling the senses—oh, what a gain!

A garden of whimsy, with joy so immense,
Each blossom's escapade is pure common sense.
So let's raise our glasses to blooms that inspire,
In this delightful chaos, we'll never tire!

Echoes of Ripeness in the Air

In the orchard, people dance,
With fruits that giggle, take a chance.
Bright red globes like cheeky sprites,
Hiding in leaves in playful bites.

Silly ladders, tumble we fall,
Chasing goodness, having a ball.
Every branch, a joyful jump,
That patch of grass—a plumpity clump.

Buzzing bees in silly hats,
These fruits must think they're acrobats.
Swinging low, they too conspire,
To dive into chaos, never tire.

As we munch on this delight,
Who knew change could taste so right?
With every giggle, we declare,
Life's a feast, let's all share!

A Palette of Possibilities

Painted red, the day is wide,
With fruity dreams we cannot hide.
Splashes of laughter, sweet surprise,
Underneath the sunny skies.

Rolling barrels, here they come,
Bouncing joy like a big drum.
Cherries popping, round they go,
Tickling toes, all in a row.

Brushes dipped in fruit-filled fun,
Creating smiles, we've just begun.
Splatters here, and drips abound,
Nature's gallery knows no bounds.

As we scribble on the ground,
Every color—joy profound.
With the laughter we ignite,
Who knew art could taste this bright?

Nature's Reflections of Hope

Mirrors in the ponds, they giggle,
Nature laughs, and we all wiggle.
Bright blooms peek from muddy streams,
Frogs join in to share our dreams.

Skipping stones, a cheeky case,
Songs of hope in every space.
A polka dot of bouncy cheer,
Sprouting giggles far and near.

Oh, the trees, they nod along,
With their branches, sing our song.
In every rustle, winds conspire,
To tickle us, we never tire.

In reflections, we find our way,
Chasing shadows, here we play.
Let's dance with whimsy, never mope,
In every glance, a leap of hope!

Harvesting Heartbeats

With baskets on our heads so high,
We reach for fruit that waves goodbye.
Each berry mocks our stretching plight,
Laughter echoes, oh what a sight!

Pies to bake or juice to make,
But first we giggle, for goodness' sake.
Muffin tops or tart delight,
Swirling sweetness, such a bite!

Tickling fingers grab with glee,
Heartbeats racing, wild and free.
Nature's gifts cause us to cheer,
Every laugh brings fruit so near.

As we munch, the sun goes down,
We wear the crowns of berry brown.
In harvest's joy, our hearts unite,
With every heartbeat, life feels bright!

Blossoms of Renewal

When life throws surprises, oh what a sight,
Like pigeons in tuxedos, taking flight.
With every new bloom, a giggle, a cheer,
We dance with the daisies, no room for fear.

A squirrel in a hat, what a curious show,
While ducks wear bowties, just so you know.
The laughter does echo with every warm breeze,
As we tumble through gardens, beneath cherry trees.

Painting our worries with colors so bright,
A jolly parade in the morning light.
With laughter as the glue for our fickle hearts,
We cook up fresh joy, life's humorous arts.

So let's skip like children, abandon the gray,
In this meadow of madness, come join the play.
For every new beginning, let's chuckle and grin,
With blossoms of whimsy, let the fun begin!

Embrace the Unseen

Invisible rabbits in fanciful shoes,
Dance through the shadows, sharing their views.
A leap and a twirl, a giggle or two,
They toast to the unseen, with pranks to pursue.

As clouds play hide-and-seek with the sun,
We chase after moments, we laugh, we run.
The serious faces we swap for a grin,
In a world full of jest, let the play begin.

With mysteries lurking around every bend,
Who knows what surprises our antics may send?
Balloons that are loose, what a jubilant flight,
Let's ride on the wind like it's pure delight.

So gather your chuckles, let joy be the theme,
In the playground of laughter, let's dance and dream.
The unseen may tickle our funny bone raw,
Life's quirks keep us smiling—let's share a guffaw!

Crimson Transformations

In a world painted crimson, where giggles take flight,
The apples wear crowns and giggle in light.
Every twist and turn is a marvelous jest,
As fruit flips the script, who laughs with the best?

Bananas in pajamas are making a scene,
While pumpkins in parties are lively and keen.
A vine full of laughter entwined with the sun,
Harvesting hilarity, oh what fun!

With each little change comes a wink and a grin,
Like strawberries waltzing with a cheeky spin.
Transformations, my friends, are never a bore,
Especially when they open up new kinds of door.

So jump in the fray, where the laughter runs wild,
Dance with the ripeness, let joy be styled.
These crimson adventures are ripe for the cause,
In the garden of giggles, let's give them applause!

Harvesting New Horizons

Plucking the fruit of tomorrow today,
With nonsense and glee, we dance and we sway.
A pickle in pigtails, what a sight to behold,
In the garden of silliness, treasures unfold.

With baskets of laughter, we gather our quirks,
Befriending the jests, where the fun always lurks.
A corn cob in shades, strutting with flair,
We harvest new horizons with giggles to spare.

Each whimsy-filled sunset paints stories on air,
As moonlight winks down, hardly a care.
Our dreams tumble forward, like apples in rolls,
In this field of amusement, we harvest our souls.

So let's dance with the seasons, with vigor and cheer,
As we celebrate changes that always draw near.
The laughter is ample, the joy never thins,
In the orchard of fun, where new life begins!

Ephemeral Blossoms

In a garden where giggles sprout,
Bumblebees buzzing, filled with doubt.
A daisy tells jokes, oh what a tease,
While tulips wiggle in the summer breeze.

One bold petal tries a dance,
Trips on roots, oh what a chance.
Laughter echoes as blooms collide,
Who's more clumsy? They can't decide.

Cultures in Bloom

A sunflower wore shades, bright and bold,
Challenging roses to share their gold.
Petunias serving tea at ten,
Crumpets with pollen, come join the zen.

The daisies debate in tiny hats,
While violets gather like sneaky spats.
Chives tell tales of the onion's tears,
While chortles rise as they sip their beers.

Cascades of Change

In a land where grapes began to play,
They threw a party to brighten the day.
Fruits in hats, oh what a sight,
Grapefruit juggled, sweet as night.

The orange danced with a twist and shout,
While apples rolled, trying to pout.
Bananas cracked jokes, oh what a bunch,
With laughs erupting, they joined the punch.

Swirling Winds of Evolution

When breezes blow like whispered sighs,
The leaves gossip, exchanging lies.
A squirrel leaps from branch to branch,
As branches giggle, they take a chance.

Winds weave tales of the butterfly,
As she flutters by with a wink and sigh.
The world spins round in a swirling twist,
Where giggling petals can't be missed.

Picking Moments of Transformation

In the orchard, laughter springs,
Where fruit winks, and the birdie sings.
A squirrel steals a shiny treat,
While we dance on our happy feet.

Baskets waiting, we act too cool,
Pretending that we're still in school.
With each pluck, a giggle flows,
As juice drips down from our toes.

Sunny faces make the best jams,
As we chat about our silly plans.
The breeze chuckles, tickling our cheeks,
While we play hide and seek with peaks.

So, let's raise a toast to the fun,
With sticky fingers, we all shall run.
Bliss blooms here, so let us play,
In nature's chaos, come what may.

The Dance of Growth in Nature's Embrace.

In fields of green, we see the shift,
Nature's jig makes our spirits lift.
Flowers bloom with every twirl,
While critters cheer in joyful whirl.

Leaves whistle tunes in the sun's glow,
As we prance like no one will know.
Every tickle from the cool breeze,
Turns our laughter into a tease.

Roots wiggle underground for fun,
While branches stretch to greet the sun.
We stumble, tumble, in our spree,
As the daisies wink, 'Come dance with me!'

So let's spin in this woodsy stage,
With froggy leaps and squirrelly rage.
In nature's arms, we find our way,
Growth is silly – come, join the play!

Ripening Seasons

Summer's here with a bubbly grin,
Fruit hangs low, let the feasting begin.
We juggle pears and tomatoes too,
As they tumble, causing quite the to-do!

Autumn's laughter cracks in the air,
Pumpkins roll over without a care.
A cornfield maze swallows our screams,
As we chase shadows and golden beams.

Winter whispers with frosty breath,
Shivering fruits dance their stealthy death.
But hope twinkles in the snowy night,
A crazy harvest brings pure delight.

Spring sneaks in with a mischievous twinkle,
As blossoms giggle and flowers crinkle.
With each season, we leap and spin,
Embrace the madness, let the fun begin!

Sweet Shifts of Nature

In the garden, giggles break the ground,
Where the funny gnomes can always be found.
With every bloom, a story's untold,
As the daisies fight for the brightest gold.

Bumblebees buzz in a drunken dance,
While butterflies join in a wild prance.
We stumble through petals, faces aglow,
Transformed by the charm of nature's show.

Bananas slip and lemons grin wide,
A comedy sketch that we can't hide.
Juicy laughter spills from our lips,
As we twirl around with wild, happy flips.

So let's toast to this wild escapade,
Where nature's giggles never do fade.
In this bloom of whimsy, let's engage,
As every shift writes a delightful page!

From Surfaces to Depths

Plucked from the tree, they take a leap,
In crumpled old baskets, they giggle and peep.
One whispers a tale, a fruity parade,
While others chime in with a juicy charade.

A pie's worth of laughter, a tart little trip,
As crumbs of adventure around us just skip.
With puns on their stems, they bounce like a ball,
Transcending all reasons, they trip and they fall.

Under the sun, they bounce and they sway,
Like jokers in costumes, they dance and they play.
Ripe with suggestions, of mischief and may,
They spin stories of joy in a most fruity way.

Fruits of the Mind

Thoughts ripe with humor, they swirl and they twist,
A brain full of nonsense, too clever to miss.
Ideas like berries hang heavy and sweet,
While giggles burst forth like a bubbly treat.

The mind takes a stroll through a vine of delight,
Where each little thought goes bloop in the night.
A puddle of chuckles, a jam full of glee,
Unruly, they tumble, just let them run free.

Like jellies and jigsaws all jumbled and rolled,
They mix in a pot, both the timid and bold.
Pour yourself a glass, take a sip of the fun,
In the garden of wisdom, the laughter's begun.

Marks of New Chapters

With scribbles and drawls, they find their own way,
Each mark a new story, a laugh in the sway.
The pages are sticky with verses that cling,
While cherries of fortune make the day sing.

Bright ink splattered dreams take flight with the breeze,
A pen full of giggles, so eager to please.
Each chapter a banquet, a feast for the mind,
Where troubles turn silly, and joy's not confined.

So open your notebook, let nonsense ignite,
With wisdom from fruit, every thought feels so light.
In the margins of laughter, new tales will take root,
Bringing smiles and delight in a quirky pursuit.

Boughs of Expansion

Swinging from branches, ideas take flight,
Like critters in costumes, they're bold and they're bright.
Twisting and turning, they wobble with cheer,
Each thought a small jester, with laughter to steer.

They stretch to the sky, breaking out of the bark,
In a playful rebellion, they steal the spotlight.
With giggles like rays shining down from the leaf,
Their antics are bold, they banish all grief.

Like taffy pulled long, or a ribbon unfurled,
Each bough brings a story to share with the world.
So come join the chatter, the fun will not cease,
In the garden of frolic, where all thoughts find peace.

Embrace the Sweetness

In a garden full of laughter,
A fruit with a wink grew shy,
It danced with a breeze so rafter,
As squirrels just laughed and hung high.

With a taste just like candy,
Each bite made us giggle so clear,
The juice dripped down quite handy,
Who knew fruit could bring such cheer?

Beneath the sun's playful glance,
We twirled with our newfound zest,
Each chuckle a bright little prance,
This fruity joy was the best!

So we shall savor the chuckles,
With every bright berry we see,
In our hearts, joy now snuggles,
Let's feast with wild glee, whee!

Transcendence in Bloom

When life gives you a berry,
Wear it as a cap, quite bold,
It might look a tad merry,
But treasures lie in the sold.

A petal fell right on my nose,
I sneezed, and the bees took flight,
Now I'm wearing pollen clothes,
Flowered fashion, quite the sight!

Twisters of colors all around,
Each hue like a giggle in air,
A parade of blooms was found,
And we danced without a care!

With fruits that could twirl and sing,
Sipping juice from a wobbly cup,
We laughed at the joy they'd bring,
In this whimsical world, we'd sup!

The Abundance of Evolution

Once a pit thought it was stuck,
In the ground, feeling quite slow,
Then came a breeze, what luck!
It sprouted legs and said, 'Let's go!'

Out in the world, it found delight,
A tangle of roots became a spree,
With buds and blooms, a dizzying sight,
'This is way better than being me!'

It flipped and flopped under the sun,
Every change was a chance to quip,
"I'm having a blast, let's have some fun!"
As a branch did a cartwheel trip!

With laughter echoing through the trees,
Nature's party was all around,
Leaves chased each other like a tease,
Who knew change could be so sound?

Fresh Pickings: Life's Opportunities

Life's a tree, ripe with tales,
Grab a fruit, avoid the gales.
Fickle winds swish as they dare,
Some fruits juicy, some quite rare.

Under sunbeams, we prance and laugh,
Chasing dreams, like a half-sharp calf.
But watch your head, don't hit a branch,
For in the trees, there's always a chance!

In the orchard, smiles abound,
With every stumble, joy is found.
Pick a thought, like cherries bright,
Flavor the world with silly delight!

So swing your basket, toss aside strife,
Snag those moments; that's the spice of life!
Unruly trees, with their quirks in tow,
Remind us to giggle, just let it flow.

Sweet Change on a Sunlit Path

Swing by the path, where shadows roam,
Sunshine giggles, beckons you home.
Surprise awaits at every turn,
With sweetened surprises, take your burn.

Stumble on flavors; a delight in disguise,
Like a pie with a twist, what a surprise!
Taste the quirks, savor the day,
With every bite, let troubles sway.

Morning dew, dancing on leaves,
With every step, mischief weaves.
Lemonade spills, oh what a scene,
A splash of joy, it's all routine!

Chasing laughter, shoes untied,
Let whimsy and wonder be your guide.
On this bright road, where jokes are cast,
Forget what's heavy, just have a blast!

Branches Bend, Spirits Soar

Branches bend with giggles loud,
Nature chuckles, gathering a crowd.
Swings of fate, oh what a ride,
Twirling fruits, laughter as our guide.

Gravity's dance, it's a playful thing,
Nature's melody, let us sing.
A twist and a turn, don't be forlorn,
Each yields a smile, where smiles are born.

Look up high, see fruits collide,
A feast of laughter, hearts open wide.
Each branch a joke, ripe for the picking,
Life's odd humor, wildly kicking!

Fluttering about, in sheer delight,
Let's celebrate what feels just right.
With branches bending, spirits in flight,
Mirth and mischief, our hearts ignite.

Serendipity in Every Scent

In the garden of oddities, I roam,
Finding scents that feel like home.
Jasmine giggles, with a hint of spice,
Silly surprises wrapped up in nice.

Fragrance dances with the breeze,
Leaves rustle softly, full of tease.
Petals chuckle as they tease my nose,
Tricky aromas in colorful rows.

Each whiff a tale, vibrant and bright,
Moments of magic taking flight.
Like candy-coated dreams, a fragrant spree,
Life's gentle nudge, wild and free!

So breathe it in and let it swirl,
In this fragrant world, let laughter twirl.
With every scent, a story cheers,
Serendipity bursts like joyous tears.

Gathering the Gold of Experience

In a world of bright confetti,
We dance on dreams, a bit unsteady.
Picking fruit from the tallest tree,
Giggling at how things can be free.

We wear our hats with silly flair,
As life throws pies, we don't despair.
Each stumble's just a quirky dance,
We spin and twirl, it's our own chance.

A lesson learned with every bite,
We laugh at wrongs that feel so right.
In the garden where joys collide,
We find the fun in every stride.

So here's to gold we've all amassed,
With laughter echoing from the past.
Each funny tale, a treasure gained,
With every bruise, we remain entertained.

Fruitful Whispers on the Wind

The breeze brings jokes from trees above,
Whispers of fun, wrapped in warm love.
As apples chuckle, pears join in,
A fruity joke that makes us grin.

Lemons laugh, while berries cheer,
Our troubles fade when joy draws near.
Lime and peach play tag all day,
With every twist, they find their way.

Mangoes fall in silly plops,
Creating laughter, the fun never stops.
In this orchard, we run and skip,
Savoring every juicy trip.

With each bite of sweet surprise,
The world gets brighter, oh how it flies!
We share the tales, we share a laugh,
In this fruit-filled, whimsical path.

Renewal in Every Bite

Take a nibble, what do you find?
A burst of joy, it's redefined.
From every fruit that brings a cheer,
A funny thought brings laughter near.

With strawberries singing silly tunes,
And grapefruits dancing by the dunes.
One tiny taste can twist the mood,
As apples snicker, feeling crude.

A pear who sings not quite in key,
Reminds us all to laugh, you see.
With every munch, a fresh delight,
Renewing spirits, taking flight.

So raise a slice, let's have a cheer,
For every bite that brings us near.
In every laugh, we find our spark,
Renewal shines, even in the dark.

The Burst of Potential Within

In the garden of dreams, we play,
Where laughs become the light of day.
A coconut's grin breaks the norm,
While grapes join in, all ripe and warm.

Each fruit holds secrets, big and small,
A burst of joy, we'll share them all.
An orange chuckles with zesty flair,
While cherries giggle, floating in air.

With every pop, ideas ignite,
Unexpected paths that feel just right.
We'll splash and dash, no need to think,
In this fruity world, we never shrink.

So here's to fun and fruity cheer,
To the bursts of life we hold so dear.
Embrace the chaos, let it spin,
For every giggle hides a win.

Blooming Potential

In the garden, sprouts so spry,
Wiggling leaves, reaching high.
A daisy dreams it's a rose,
While a weed just strikes a pose.

Petals sing in a daylight romp,
A daffodil doing the happy stomp.
Around the bend, a gnome with flair,
Trying to style his wild, wild hair.

Weather them winds, with giggles so bright,
Seeds of laughter take their flight.
Gathering clouds for a silly dance,
Nature's stage, come take a chance!

So let's grow wild, be weird and bold,
In this garden, stories unfold.
With every bloom, a chuckle we find,
In every sprout, joy intertwined.

The Flavor of Transformation

In a stew of emotions, mix it well,
Add a dash of laughter, give it a swell.
Salt the tears and stir the dreams,
Cook up life in fanciful themes.

Fruits of wisdom hang from the vine,
Mangoes play tricks, oh, how they shine!
Spinach giggles while dressed in green,
It's the funniest salad we've ever seen!

Sifting through flavors, zest and cheer,
Tasting life, with friends near.
Life's a banquet, don't you see?
A dash of humor sets you free!

Stir it sweet, or maybe tart,
Every flavor plays a part.
So raise a glass to silly delights,
Laughing through our foodie nights.

Cherry Hues of Tomorrow

A canvas bright, a painter's tease,
Colors splatter with the greatest ease.
In this madness where hues collide,
Smudged with giggles, we'll take a ride.

Bubbles float in a rainbow sky,
While squirrels debate, why donuts fly.
Dancing shades, a tricky affair,
Red is shy, and green pulls hair!

In the land of fruit and fun,
Where jellybeans twirl just for a pun.
Let's paint a world that makes us grin,
With every twist, let the fun begin!

Fuzzy fluffy clouds are low,
Eager to join our colorful show.
So grab your brush, let's paint the dream,
Tomorrow's hues burst at the seam!

Awakening Reverie

Awake I am to a morning spree,
Where coffee chats with a bumblebee.
A whistle from a kettle springs,
As toast debates with fruit on swings.

Socks mismatched, a fashion faux pas,
Ping pong balls in a game of cha-cha.
Waffles giggle at syrup's grace,
As doughnuts roll, the faster the race!

Tickle the dawn with playful cheer,
Yesterday's blues all disappear.
With every wink of the sun's soft eye,
Life laughs, twirls, and waves goodbye.

In this dreamscape, let's sway and sway,
Embrace the funny in every day.
Awakened moments, sprightly and free,
Dance with joy, 'tis the key!

Harvesting Hope

In the garden of dreams, we find our glee,
Plucking ideas like fruit, so happily.
With baskets of laughter, we gather the day,
Who knew hopes could ripen in such a fun way?

We twist and we turn, in the sunshine so bright,
Like silly old squirrels, we dance with delight.
Each bloom a wild joke, a vibrant slight tease,
Oh, laughter is ripe, like the sweetest of peas.

We shake up the branches, don't mind a few spills,
Harvesting giggles, we start up the thrills.
With arms full of smiles, we skip down the lane,
Taking life lightly like an orange in rain.

So, let's fill our hats with the joy that we find,
In fields of imagination, we're wonderfully blind.
With each cheeky chuckle, our hopes on a swing,
We're harvesting happiness, oh what a fling!

Bountiful Horizons

In a land where the sun makes the sillies grow,
We chase after visions like a zany rainbow.
With wind in our hair, we leap high and free,
Filling pockets with daydreams, under the tree.

The clouds start to giggle, the flowers all cheer,
As we bounce through the fields, nothing to fear.
With each little twirl, we plant seeds of cheer,
The horizon is bright, can you see it appear?

Like popcorn on corn cobs, ideas just pop,
We gather and grow, there's no need to stop.
A carousel of colors spinning around,
In this bountiful place, pure joy can be found.

With baskets of laughter, we skip and we sway,
Each moment a treasure, come giggle and play.
So tip your hat forward, let's dive into fun,
In this wild garden, we're never outrun!

Vibrations of Change

The world does a jig in its quirky old way,
Like a cat on a roof at the break of the day.
Each tremor a joke that shakes up our minds,
Turning upside-down, what thrill that it finds!

With a wiggle and squirm, we dance out of time,
In puddles of laughter, we splash and we chime.
The winds play a tune, so silly and bright,
As we cha-cha the hours, from morning to night.

Just when we thought life had gone off the rails,
The wobbles of fate send us laughter-filled trails.
With hiccups of joy, and a snort or a squeal,
We find the weird wonders that life has to steal.

So let's ride the waves of these vibrant strange beats,
Squeezing life's juice, oh, what tasty treats!
In this carnival dance, we embrace the wild range,
Swinging high on the swings of those bright vibrations of change.

The Aroma of Growth

In a pot filled with humor, seeds ready to sprout,
We breathe in the giggles, that's what it's about.
With sprinkles of sunshine, and water of cheer,
We raise up our noses, the sweet scent is near.

The garden is buzzing with funny old bees,
Who hum a bright tune as they buzz through the leaves.
With every new petal that starts to unfurl,
A dance of delight, like a candy swirl.

Oh, how the compost delivers the best,
A banquet of laughter, nature's merry fest.
With each twist and turn, we're crafting new schemes,
In the aroma of growth, we're living in dreams.

Let's sprinkle some spice on this journey we take,
Find joy in the soil, and dance with the quake.
With each little bloom, let's tickle the air,
In this fragrant adventure, let's go everywhere!

Fruits of Evolution

Once a green apple, quite out of style,
Now turns into pears, with a cheeky smile.
Bananas now dancing, or so it seems,
They're plotting on trees, crafting their dreams.

Caught a grape giggling, said 'I'm a star,'
Sassy and sweet, with a hint of bizarre.
Lemons in line for a stylish makeover,
Zesty they whisper, 'We're ready for flavor!'

Coconuts chuckle up in the trees,
Waving their husks in the tropical breeze.
An orange claims it can sing like a tune,
But it sounds more like a fruit-laden moon.

A fig in the corner, claiming it's wise,
Says evolution came with a side of fries.
So let's all embrace this fruity parade,
For change can be funny, and never delayed!

Whispers of Growth

In the garden of giggles, seeds were once sown,
Radishes wearing tiny hats made of stone.
Carrots with manners, they stand in a line,
Bragging how juicy, they'll soon be divine.

Herbs gossip softly, 'Did you hear that?'
Mint is planning a party; how's that for a spat?
Basil is blushing, too shy to be bold,
While dill flirts with flowers, oh, if truth be told!

Tomatoes in shades of red and of green,
Argue who's juicier, but what a routine!
Onions just sulk in their layers of tears,
While peppers take selfies, enjoying their years.

Each sprout a comedian, growing their way,
Growing is fun, let's all join the play!
So raise up a toast with a fruit or a sprout,
For growth can be funny, without any doubt!

The Spice of New Beginnings

Cinnamon giggles, igniting a spark,
Says, 'Let's spice life up, come dance in the dark!'
Nutmeg grins slyly, 'I may be quite round,
But watch me get fancy, when I'm finely ground.'

Paprika's flamboyant, it loves to be seen,
Cayenne is hotter than a sunken submarine.
Ginger, the prankster, offers a zest,
With a wink and a spin, it takes on the quest.

Saffron's a diva, all decked out in gold,
While cardamom whispers, 'I'm quirky and bold!'
They gather together, a spice rack so grand,
Laughing and brewing, oh, isn't it planned?

Through all the confusion, they flavor our plates,
Adding some humor, 'Let's spice up our fates!'
With laughter and fragrance, let's make a new turn,
For beginnings are tasty, it's our time to learn!

Echoes of the Blossom

A daisy declared in a voice loud and clear,
'With blossoms around, there's nothing to fear!'
Tulips take selfies, in bright colors bloom,
While sunflowers wink, lifting up their own gloom.

Roses just chuckle, in shades red and pink,
They ponder their thorns—'Just a cute little wink!'
Violets are modest, hiding back in the crowd,
Yet their giggles are mighty: go ahead, be loud!

Daffodils frolic, in spring's sunny light,
Chasing the bees with all of their might.
Cherry blossoms whisper of change to be made,
In each joyful petal, a new truth conveyed.

As laughter erupts in the soft morning dew,
Together they flourish, this crew, oh so true!
In gardens of humor, where all can find grace,
For echoes can tickle, and change's a warm place!

Cultivating Tomorrow

In the garden of laughter, seeds we sow,
Giggling with gnomes, racing the crow.
With watering cans, we splash and we play,
Growing a crop that's silly and gay.

Sunshine smiles down, and clouds throw a jest,
We'll cultivate joy in our funny fest.
Radishes dance, while carrots all cheer,
Tomorrow will be bright, never fear!

Jellybeans sprout, and lollipops sway,
Planting our dreams in a rainbow array.
With chatter of critters, the squirrels drop by,
While bees buzz in tune, oh my, oh my!

So let's plant a joke, and let laughter bloom,
In this orchard of quirks, there's always more room.
For every giggle, a tree grows, you see,
Cultivating tomorrow with glee and esprit!

The Journey of Flavor

On a ride through the pods of flavor so bright,
I hopped on a berry that took off in flight.
Racing with pickles, we zoomed past the pies,
Searching for giggles beneath the blue skies.

We landed in salsa, a party so grand,
With dancing cucumbers, we sang hand in hand.
Avocados were spinning, they hummed a sweet tune,
While tomatoes did cartwheels beneath the bright moon.

A zest of excitement, a sprinkle of cheer,
Jellyfish jazz playing, let's dance, my dear!
Through forests of flavors, we traveled with glee,
This journey of taste, oh what fun it will be!

So grab your forks, friends, don't delay,
Let's munch on the fun in a whimsical way.
Every bite tells a tale that will surely amaze,
Flavor's a journey, let's sing its praise!

Reflections in the Orchard

In the orchard of mischief, I found quite the sight,
A mirror of laughter where fruits took flight.
Bananas wearing hats, oh what a view,
Cherries are giggling, as berries break through.

Grapes start to gossip, seeds spill their tea,
With each juicy story, how fun it can be!
The apples just wink, with a sparkle so bright,
While coconuts chuckle, oh what a delight!

A dance with the pears, a jive with the figs,
Where laughter and sweetness perform little jigs.
Mirror, mirror, what do you see?
Reflections of joy, how silly and free!

So let's enjoy this quirky display,
Of fruits filled with laughter, brightening our day.
In this orchard of whimsy, we find what we seek,
Every giggle a treasure, every joke unique!

Harvested Dreams

Under the moonlight, we gather the fun,
With baskets of laughter, our work has begun.
Carrots in costumes, they shout with delight,
As we harvest our dreams on this magical night.

Tomatoes do cartwheels, radishes grin,
While pumpkins tell secrets, let the giggles begin.
We pick up the joy, tossing jokes in the air,
Each chuckle we gather, a harvest rare!

The harvest festival dances, the night's in full swing,
The fruits tell their tales, oh the joy they bring!
With every sweet bite, let's cheers all around,
To laughter and dreams, let's spread the joy found.

So gather your friends, let's eat and let's play,
In the orchard of laughter, we'll dance till the day.
For every sweet moment, a dream we can glean,
In this funny old harvest, we're living the dream!

Orchard of Possibilities

In a grove where giggles grow,
Kooky fruits put on a show.
They wobble, jiggle, take a chance,
Inviting all to join the dance.

Ants wear hats, squirrels wear ties,
As fruit debates under sunny skies.
Peaches argue with a plump pear,
"I'm juicier!" they shout with flair.

Lemons laugh at the sweet displays,
Juggling zest in comical ways.
Apples roll, showing off their style,
"Bet you can't keep up!" they smile.

In this orchard, dreams are spry,
Every fruit sings, never shy.
Make a wish, let laughter bloom,
In this garden, there's always room.

From Bud to Bloom: A Journey

A little bud in the morning light,
Said, "I'll be a flower, oh what a sight!"
But slipped on dew, with a comedic flair,
And landed in mud with a squishy stare.

The stem shook off the muddy coat,
"Just wait until I'm on a float!"
With petals bright, like a rainbow's fail,
A bee buzzed by—"You'll soon set sail!"

Later blooms played dress-up bold,
In hats of petals, stories told.
"Who looks the silliest?" they agreed,
While laughing, they danced with grace and speed.

As evening fell with skies aglow,
The flower showed off one hilarious toe.
Life's a journey, spicy and fun,
Just like that bud—its race is won!

Transformation Tastes Like Summer

A sprout woke up with a sunny grin,
"Watch me sprout, unstoppable kin!"
But tripped on roots in the garden bed,
Looking silly, it danced instead.

Watering can sang its happy tune,
"Keep growing! Be a fruit, not a prune!"
As laughter echoed, the garden blushed,
Each blossom grew nervous, but then, they rushed.

Summer scents mixed with a twist,
"Let's create a smoothie!" all fruits insisted.
In a blender they flew, a berry parade,
Chunky or smooth, they just couldn't fade.

A feast of giggles filled the air,
With wild concoctions made with flair.
To transform is to sprout some cheer,
Each sip a laugh, kicking off the year!

The Taste of Tomorrow's Sunrise

A sprightly sunrise burst forth today,
With fruity shades that dance and play.
Cherries winked, with mischief in tow,
"Let's sneak a taste of what we know!"

Bananas slipped on sticky bliss,
"Upside down? Oh, that's pure miss!"
Oranges rolled down the gentle hill,
"Catch me if you can!" a zesty thrill.

Morning dew dripped like sweetened song,
"Join the breakfast party; it won't be long!"
As muffins giggled, toast did jive,
In this kitchen, all are alive.

So savor each chuckle, each juicy cheer,
Tomorrow's sunrise is always near.
Taste the fun, let flavors collide,
In each bite, let laughter reside.

Ripening Dreams in Autumn's Embrace

Beneath the tree, dreams play hide and seek,
Falling down like fruity confetti, so bleak.
Squirrels dance in a zany parade,
Catching their snacks, hoping to be paid.

With each plop and a laughter-filled cheer,
I ponder my choices, oh dear, oh dear!
Look at them roll, a wild chase ensues,
My life's like a sitcom, wearing mismatched shoes.

In the harvest of giggles, joy takes its stand,
An absurd buffet created by nature's hand.
Plucking the ripened, sharing the fun,
With each fruity bite, we all come undone.

So let's toast to the seasons, in shades bold and bright,
Where dreams get a chance in the autumnal light.
I'll chase after thrills, as the world spins around,
In the orchard of nonsense, true laughter is found.

Petals Fall, Futures Rise

Petals tumble like comedians in flight,
Spinning and twirling, what a silly sight!
With each gentle gust, they tumble and sway,
Turning the garden into a stage play.

Futures rise with a pop and a twist,
An unplanned routine, who could have guessed?
Bees buzzing in tune, like drummers in glee,
While flowers sing songs about being free.

Laughter erupts as new colors collide,
Butterflies giggle, nowhere to hide.
A humorous dance, the blooms know their part,
Whispering secrets of change with great heart.

In the chaos of petals, there's wisdom to glean,
With laughter we flourish, it's all quite a scene.
So let's lift our glasses, to seasons anew,
Where humor and nature delight in their view.

Juicy Promises in the Breeze

A breeze brings a message, so juicy, so bright,
Promises wrapped in laughter take flight.
In the orchard we giggle, with branches a-sway,
At the buffet of life, come join in the fray!

With every ripe fruit comes a story or two,
Of slips and of trips and a wacky debut.
Frolicking critters, oh what a parade,
Life's juicy mishaps, how they've been made!

Each bite a reminder of moments gone by,
The sweet and the sour, oh my, oh my!
We share in the laughter, the flavor of fun,
As sunlight and joy blend into one.

So let's toss our worries into the high trees,
Embrace every giggle, let's dance in the breeze.
In the orchard of change, we're forever entwined,
With juicy sweet promises, humor defined.

When Summer Leaves, We Blossom

Summer waves goodbye with a playful grin,
Leaves us with memories of games tucked within.
As autumn steps in, with a skip and a hop,
New blooms burst forth, we just can't stop!

Dancing with colors, we spin and we twirl,
Each petal a giggle, in a whimsical swirl.
With the breeze as our partner, we leap in delight,
Tomorrow holds promise, so let's take flight!

Squirrels are plotting their cheeky escapes,
Nature's comedians in mismatched capes.
As we wave under branches, watch our worries dissolve,
In this silly world, together we evolve.

So here's to bright blooms when the heat starts to fade,
A season for laughing and fun we've all made.
When summer leaves us, we blossom with cheer,
In this garden of nonsense, let's spread love far and near.

Melodies of Metamorphosis

In springtime's dance, a twist of fate,
With buzzing bees, and laughter great.
A hat made of leaves, a rabbit's grin,
Who's changing who? Let's spin to win!

The wind hums tunes of silly pranks,
As flowers jest, and nature wanks.
Oh, watch as caterpillars strut,
In disco balls, they're in a rut!

The sun plays tricks, a game of shade,
With dappled spots, no one's afraid.
The breeze tickles everyone here,
As giggles swell, and doubts disappear!

So join the fun, let the world see,
That changing shapes can be the key.
With every twist, a new delight,
In metamorphosis, we take flight!

Turning Leaves

A rustle here, a flap of leaves,
Who knew they had such crafty schemes?
They spin and swoop like dizzy sprites,
In autumn's game of wild delights!

One leaf wore boots, another a hat,
They twirled and tumbled, oh how they sat!
Hoping to catch a squirrel's eye,
To join their dance, oh me, oh my!

A nutmeg joke, a pumpkin pun,
The laughter echoed, 'til day was done.
With every gust, they'd leap and soar,
Each turning leaf craved more and more!

So gather round, let spirits rise,
In swirling colors beneath the skies.
For in this game, we're all involved,
With nature's whims, we're truly solved!

Turning Lives

In bustling streets, the bodies twist,
Each person caught in life's own list.
With coffee cups and crazy hats,
They dance through days like laughing cats!

One stumbles on a shoelace trap,
A giggle bursts, and off they clap.
Around the corner, a dance-off starts,
As old folks join with youthful hearts!

With juggling dreams and spinning hopes,
They paint the world like kaleidoscopes.
Each life a story, layered bright,
In turning tales, we find our light!

So lift your chin, embrace the fun,
With every twist, we are becoming one.
In this grand waltz, we break our strife,
Together we dance, embracing life!

The Color of Awakening

From slumber deep, the world awakes,
In colors bold, the laughter quakes.
A sleepy sun peeks through the mist,
While flowers bloom, they can't resist!

The trees wear socks, and squirrels giggle,
With springtime pranks, they dance and wiggle.
A parade of petals, the colors clash,
As bees hop over in a buzzing flash!

But wait, what's that? A grumpy bear,
And pie in his paw with a delightful stare.
He snorts a tune with berry flair,
While we all join in without a care!

With joy embraced, the world ignites,
As every day brings new delights.
In this canvas where we play and sing,
Awakening joy is the sweetest thing!

Time's Vibrant Palette

Each tick a splash, a brushstroke bright,
With every hour, there's pure delight.
The hands of time paint skies in blue,
While green frogs leap, just wait and view!

A daisy wears a funky tie,
As clouds parade by in the sky.
Tick-tock goes the playful clock,
With giggling chimes, it surely rocks!

The colors blend in harmony,
With laughter swirling joyfully.
In every second, change takes flight,
With vibrant hues, it feels so right!

So grab your brush, let joy unfurl,
In this grand scheme, let laughter whirl.
For life's a canvas, wild and free,
In time's grand dance, just laugh with glee!

Rippling Tides of Time

Time is a wave that loves to surf,
Riding the ripples, causing a smurf.
Tick-tock, tick-tock, the clocks go wild,
Like a playful puppy, just a silly child.

We count our years like kids count sheep,
With wishes and dreams, and a laugh, we leap.
Each second slips by like ice cream on toast,
A sticky delight that we cherish the most.

Swirling around, the past gives a wink,
Mixing the colors of what we think.
A memory pops, a giggle or two,
Suddenly life feels like a party for you!

So let's toast to change, let spirits ignite,
With chuckles and cheers, we take flight tonight.
As tides roll and shift, we wave our goodbyes,
In the ocean of moments, where laughter never dies.

Radiant Red Awakening

In the morning light, the fruits come alive,
Red as a clown's nose, oh how they thrive!
A dance of delight in the orchard's embrace,
Where juice flows like laughter, oh what a place!

The color so bright, it brings a chuckle,
Like a jester in court, causing a shuffle.
Unruly, these berries, in riotous hues,
They jiggle and wiggle, with nothing to lose.

With baskets in hand, we gather the joy,
Like kids with new toys, no cares to destroy.
Each bite bursts with mirth, a silly parade,
Making even the grumpiest hearts feel unafraid.

So let's raise a toast to the fun we create,
With fruit in our hands, let's laugh while we wait.
In this radiant garden, where jesters play,
A red awakening brings us bright, funny days!

Petals of Possibility

Petals flutter down, like whispers of fate,
In the breeze of ideas, where giggles await.
Colors collide in a glorious mess,
Painting the world with a comical dress.

Each flower a dream with its own silly twist,
A bloom that remembers, it simply can't resist.
Bouncing and bobbing, they dance on the breeze,
With quirky intentions, they aim to please.

In gardens of laughter, we wander and jest,
With petals of promise, we craft our own quest.
A hornet in bloom plays the prankster's role,
Tickling our fancies, it steals the whole show.

So gather your petals, share chuckles and cheer,
For in each little laugh, life's magic draws near.
In the garden of whimsy, let's drift and let go,
In the petals of possibility, let joy overflow!

A Shift in the Orchard

In the orchard today, a shift in the air,
Trees whisper secrets with comical flair.
Branches creak and sway like they're dancing a jig,
While squirrels in costumes put on quite the gig!

The apples take bets on who'll drop to the ground,
While pears roll their eyes, saying, "Look at them clown!"

With puns in their cores and laughter so ripe,
Each fruit's an acrobat in this playful hype.

A ripe raspberry chuckles, 'I'm the sweetest of all!'
While cherries argue, "No, I'm the belle of the ball!"
In a twist of hilarity, a grape slips and trips,
Sending all of them tumbling in whimsical flips.

So let's join the fun in this orchard so grand,
Where shifts and surprises run wild on demand.
With giggles and grins, we'll dance through the grove,
In this playful paradise, let's all lose and rove!

Tasting Change

I bit a fruit quite sweet and round,
It giggled softly as I found.
The juice dripped down my chin with glee,
It laughed and said, "Come taste with me!"

I swapped my soda for this delight,
It winked at me, oh what a sight!
Once a couch potato, now I roam,
With every bite, I start to comb.

The flavor danced, it wiggled so,
A fruity jig, a vibrant show!
I think I'm part fruit now, who knew?
A cherry giggle, that's my cue!

Let's toast to fruits, to lively prance,
With juicy smiles, we'll take a chance!
Each crunch a hint of wild, bright cheer,
I'll never be a potato, dear!

From Bud to Bloom

A little bud peeped out, so shy,
'Oh dear,' it said, 'I'm afraid to try.'
But sunbeams tickled it awake,
'Bloom, darling bud, for laughter's sake!'

It stretched and giggled, petals grew,
A vibrant dance, a playful view.
With every breeze, it tossed and twirled,
'This blooming life? I'm quite unfurled!'

Then came the bee, all buzzing mad,
'You look so lovely, I'm not bad!'
They twirled together, a comical sight,
A blooming romance, oh what a night!

From shy little bud to colorful show,
A waltz through gardens, what joy to glow!
With giggles and pollen, they both did zoom,
A tale of cheer shaped every bloom!

Lush Landscapes of Tomorrow

In fields where troubles used to sprout,
Now joy and laughter skip about.
Once barren lands of frowns and sighs,
Are now a palette of bright blue skies.

A kite flew by, its tail was long,
It danced with clouds, a playful song.
'Look at me soar!' it hollered loud,
'No more the grumpy, sullen crowd!'

The trees did shimmy, leaves a-blur,
With squirrels wearing hats, what a stir!
They pranced on branches, cheeky and bold,
In this lush land, new tales unfold.

Bright colors splash where gloom went down,
Every corner wears a jolly crown.
A landscape rich with funny sights,
Where tomorrow blooms, and laughter lights!

Unraveling Threads of Past

I found a sweater from long ago,
It had a story, wouldn't you know?
With pockets deep, and stitches old,
It whispered tales that made me bold.

I pulled the yarn and gave a tug,
Out popped a cat, a laughing rug!
'You knit me tight, now watch me roam,
Unravel these threads, let's find a home!'

Around we danced, a comical spree,
As tangled memories set us free.
Each stitch unwound, we laughed and spun,
Revisiting moments, oh what fun!

So here's to pasts that tickle our toes,
To yarns unwound and laughter that flows.
With every thread, a story shines,
Unraveled joys, like wild designs!

The Weight of New Fruits

A ladder creaks as I reach high,
Picking plump dreams from the branches nearby.
The fruit is ripe, heavy as a thought,
I wonder what wisdom this harvest has brought.

Juggling my thoughts in a basket of glee,
One slips away, it rolls past my knee.
With laughter I chase it, barefoot and bold,
Who knew wise ideas could be so uncontrolled?

The bushes are whispering secrets untold,
They tease with bright colors, enticing and bold.
I snack on my choices, the juicy delight,
Taking bites out of future, with every small bite.

So, here's to the harvest of giggles and gaffs,
Weighty ideas that lead to big laughs.
If life gives you fruit, then wear it like crowns,
And let all your worries tumble down like clowns.

Bursts of Epiphany

A fruit tree shaking with raucous delight,
Gives bursts of bright colors, a humorous sight.
I pluck a ripe orange, it slips from my grip,
Rolls down the sidewalk, oh what a trip!

I ponder my thoughts as it dances away,
Maybe it's wise to let laughter sway.
Each citrusy tumble, a message so clear,
Don't take life too seriously, just crack a cheer!

Suddenly lemons join in on the fun,
Their sour expressions speak, "Why so glum?"
A zesty parade, marching to the light,
Who knew enlightenment could taste so bright?

In the end, I find joy in the fruit's crazy dance,
A lesson in laughter, in each little chance.
So roll with the giggles, and savor that zest,
Because life's little moments are truly the best!

Weaving the Future

Threads of bright berries, tangled and sweet,
I weave them together, a luscious treat.
Each stitch a thought, a vision that's spry,
With laughter and color, it twirls in the sky.

A tapestry grows, a wild patchwork view,
Berries jostle and giggle, that's what they do.
They whisper to me, 'Don't worry the hours,
Just blend in the fun, sprinkle with flowers!'

Unruly vines weave a whimsical trail,
Like hiccups in laughter that pitter and pale.
I twine in my dreams, let each fruity hue,
Show how to dance lightly, as breezes flow through.

In this odd mix, I find joy anew,
Who knew tangled tales could feel this askew?
So here's to the weaving of futures so bright,
With fruity confetti, I take off in flight!

Tints of Transition

A rainbow of fruits hangs low in the air,
Each plump sphere giggles, 'No reason to despair!'
The cherries are blushing, all decked out in hue,
While kiwi chimes in, 'We're awesome, it's true!'

With every expression, there's humor to find,
Transitions are tasty, so playful and kind.
Mangoes in sandals proclaim it's all good,
'Join us in laughter, it's a fruitful mood!'

The tints keep on shifting, from green into gold,
Each color a giggle, a story retold.
Outrageous and vivid, they pop and they sway,
Transitions are tasty, come join in the play!

So raise up your glasses to transitions so fine,
Where fruits of our labor can spark and can shine.
With laughter like bubbles, let's savor the thrill,
For life's a good harvest, and laughter's the still!

www.ingramcontent.com/pod-product-compliance
Lightning Source LLC
Chambersburg PA
CBHW060115230426
43661CB00003B/186